Budget It!

The Little Book For Keeping Track of Book Costs

Created & Designed By
TeeCee Design Studio

Book Title: _______________________________

Editing:

Formatting:

Cover:

Promotional Graphics:

Blog Tours:

Swag:

Gifts:

Print Copies:

Ad/Promotions:

Other Costs:

Total Costs:

Book Title: _______________________________

Editing:

Formatting:

Cover:

Promotional Graphics:

Blog Tours:

Swag:

Gifts:

Print Copies:

Ad/Promotions:

Other Costs:

Total Costs:

Book Title: _______________________________

Editing:

Formatting:

Cover:

Promotional Graphics:

Blog Tours:

Swag:

Gifts:

Print Copies:

Ad/Promotions:

Other Costs:

Total Costs:

Book Title: _______________________________

Editing:

Formatting:

Cover:

Promotional Graphics:

Blog Tours:

Swag:

Gifts:

Print Copies:

Ad/Promotions:

Other Costs:

Total Costs:

Book Title: _________________________________

Editing:

Formatting:

Cover:

Promotional Graphics:

Blog Tours:

Swag:

Gifts:

Print Copies:

Ad/Promotions:

Other Costs:

Total Costs:

Book Title: ___________________________________

Editing:

Formatting:

Cover:

Promotional Graphics:

Blog Tours:

Swag:

Gifts:

Print Copies:

Ad/Promotions:

Other Costs:

Total Costs:

Book Title: ___________________________________

Editing: [ ]

Formatting: [ ]

Cover: [ ]

Promotional Graphics: [ ]

Blog Tours: [ ]

Swag: [ ]

Gifts: [ ]

Print Copies: [ ]

Ad/Promotions: [ ]

Other Costs:

_______________ [ ]   _______________ [ ]

_______________ [ ]   _______________ [ ]

_______________ [ ]   _______________ [ ]

_______________ [ ]   _______________ [ ]

_______________ [ ]   _______________ [ ]

Total Costs: [ ]

Book Title: _______________________________

Editing:

Formatting:

Cover:

Promotional Graphics:

Blog Tours:

Swag:

Gifts:

Print Copies:

Ad/Promotions:

Other Costs:

Total Costs:

Book Title: _________________________________

Editing:

Formatting:

Cover:

Promotional Graphics:

Blog Tours:

Swag:

Gifts:

Print Copies:

Ad/Promotions:

Other Costs:

Total Costs:

Book Title: _______________________________

Editing:

Formatting:

Cover:

Promotional Graphics:

Blog Tours:

Swag:

Gifts:

Print Copies:

Ad/Promotions:

Other Costs:

Total Costs:

Book Title: _______________________________

Editing:

Formatting:

Cover:

Promotional Graphics:

Blog Tours:

Swag:

Gifts:

Print Copies:

Ad/Promotions:

Other Costs:

Total Costs:

Book Title: _______________________________

Editing:

Formatting:

Cover:

Promotional Graphics:

Blog Tours:

Swag:

Gifts:

Print Copies:

Ad/Promotions:

Other Costs:

Total Costs:

Book Title: _______________________________

Editing:

Formatting:

Cover:

Promotional Graphics:

Blog Tours:

Swag:

Gifts:

Print Copies:

Ad/Promotions:

Other Costs:

Total Costs:

Book Title: _______________________________

Editing:

Formatting:

Cover:

Promotional Graphics:

Blog Tours:

Swag:

Gifts:

Print Copies:

Ad/Promotions:

Other Costs:

Total Costs:

Book Title: ______________________________

Editing:

Formatting:

Cover:

Promotional Graphics:

Blog Tours:

Swag:

Gifts:

Print Copies:

Ad/Promotions:

Other Costs:

Total Costs:

Book Title: _______________________________

Editing:

Formatting:

Cover:

Promotional Graphics:

Blog Tours:

Swag:

Gifts:

Print Copies:

Ad/Promotions:

Other Costs:

Total Costs:

Book Title: _______________________________

Editing:

Formatting:

Cover:

Promotional Graphics:

Blog Tours:

Swag:

Gifts:

Print Copies:

Ad/Promotions:

Other Costs:

Total Costs:

Book Title: _______________________________

Editing:

Formatting:

Cover:

Promotional Graphics:

Blog Tours:

Swag:

Gifts:

Print Copies:

Ad/Promotions:

Other Costs:

Total Costs:

Book Title: _______________________________

Editing: [ ]

Formatting: [ ]

Cover: [ ]

Promotional Graphics: [ ]

Blog Tours: [ ]

Swag: [ ]

Gifts: [ ]

Print Copies: [ ]

Ad/Promotions: [ ]

Other Costs:

_______________	[ ]	_______________	[ ]
_______________	[ ]	_______________	[ ]
_______________	[ ]	_______________	[ ]
_______________	[ ]	_______________	[ ]
_______________	[ ]	_______________	[ ]

Total Costs: [ ]

Book Title: _______________________________

Editing:

Formatting:

Cover:

Promotional Graphics:

Blog Tours:

Swag:

Gifts:

Print Copies:

Ad/Promotions:

Other Costs:

Total Costs:

Book Title: _______________________________

Editing:

Formatting:

Cover:

Promotional Graphics:

Blog Tours:

Swag:

Gifts:

Print Copies:

Ad/Promotions:

Other Costs:

Total Costs:

Book Title: _______________________________

Editing:

Formatting:

Cover:

Promotional Graphics:

Blog Tours:

Swag:

Gifts:

Print Copies:

Ad/Promotions:

Other Costs:

Total Costs:

Book Title: ___________________________________

Editing:

Formatting:

Cover:

Promotional Graphics:

Blog Tours:

Swag:

Gifts:

Print Copies:

Ad/Promotions:

Other Costs:

Total Costs:

Book Title: ________________________________

Editing:

Formatting:

Cover:

Promotional Graphics:

Blog Tours:

Swag:

Gifts:

Print Copies:

Ad/Promotions:

Other Costs:

Total Costs:

Book Title: _______________________________

Editing:

Formatting:

Cover:

Promotional Graphics:

Blog Tours:

Swag:

Gifts:

Print Copies:

Ad/Promotions:

Other Costs:

Total Costs:

Book Title: ______________________________

Editing:

Formatting:

Cover:

Promotional Graphics:

Blog Tours:

Swag:

Gifts:

Print Copies:

Ad/Promotions:

Other Costs:

Total Costs:

Book Title: _______________________________

Editing:

Formatting:

Cover:

Promotional Graphics:

Blog Tours:

Swag:

Gifts:

Print Copies:

Ad/Promotions:

Other Costs:

Total Costs:

Book Title: _______________________________

Editing:

Formatting:

Cover:

Promotional Graphics:

Blog Tours:

Swag:

Gifts:

Print Copies:

Ad/Promotions:

Other Costs:

Total Costs:

Book Title: _______________________________

Editing:

Formatting:

Cover:

Promotional Graphics:

Blog Tours:

Swag:

Gifts:

Print Copies:

Ad/Promotions:

Other Costs:

Total Costs:

Book Title: ______________________________

Editing:

Formatting:

Cover:

Promotional Graphics:

Blog Tours:

Swag:

Gifts:

Print Copies:

Ad/Promotions:

Other Costs:

Total Costs:

Book Title: _________________________________

Editing:

Formatting:

Cover:

Promotional Graphics:

Blog Tours:

Swag:

Gifts:

Print Copies:

Ad/Promotions:

Other Costs:

Total Costs:

Book Title: ______________________________

Editing:

Formatting:

Cover:

Promotional Graphics:

Blog Tours:

Swag:

Gifts:

Print Copies:

Ad/Promotions:

Other Costs:

Total Costs:

Book Title: _______________________________

Editing:

Formatting:

Cover:

Promotional Graphics:

Blog Tours:

Swag:

Gifts:

Print Copies:

Ad/Promotions:

Other Costs:

Total Costs:

Book Title: ______________________________

Editing:

Formatting:

Cover:

Promotional Graphics:

Blog Tours:

Swag:

Gifts:

Print Copies:

Ad/Promotions:

Other Costs:

Total Costs:

Book Title: _______________________________

Editing:

Formatting:

Cover:

Promotional Graphics:

Blog Tours:

Swag:

Gifts:

Print Copies:

Ad/Promotions:

Other Costs:

Total Costs:

Book Title: _______________________________

Editing:

Formatting:

Cover:

Promotional Graphics:

Blog Tours:

Swag:

Gifts:

Print Copies:

Ad/Promotions:

Other Costs:

Total Costs:

Book Title: _______________________________

Editing:

Formatting:

Cover:

Promotional Graphics:

Blog Tours:

Swag:

Gifts:

Print Copies:

Ad/Promotions:

Other Costs:

Total Costs:

Book Title: _______________________________

Editing:

Formatting:

Cover:

Promotional Graphics:

Blog Tours:

Swag:

Gifts:

Print Copies:

Ad/Promotions:

Other Costs:

Total Costs:

Book Title: ________________________________

Editing: [ ]

Formatting: [ ]

Cover: [ ]

Promotional Graphics: [ ]

Blog Tours: [ ]

Swag: [ ]

Gifts: [ ]

Print Copies: [ ]

Ad/Promotions: [ ]

Other Costs:

____________ [ ]   ____________ [ ]

____________ [ ]   ____________ [ ]

____________ [ ]   ____________ [ ]

____________ [ ]   ____________ [ ]

____________ [ ]   ____________ [ ]

Total Costs: [ ]

Book Title: ________________________________

Editing:

Formatting:

Cover:

Promotional Graphics:

Blog Tours:

Swag:

Gifts:

Print Copies:

Ad/Promotions:

Other Costs:

Total Costs:

Book Title: _______________________________

Editing:

Formatting:

Cover:

Promotional Graphics:

Blog Tours:

Swag:

Gifts:

Print Copies:

Ad/Promotions:

Other Costs:

Total Costs:

Book Title: _______________________________

Editing:

Formatting:

Cover:

Promotional Graphics:

Blog Tours:

Swag:

Gifts:

Print Copies:

Ad/Promotions:

Other Costs:

Total Costs:

Book Title: ____________________________

Editing:

Formatting:

Cover:

Promotional Graphics:

Blog Tours:

Swag:

Gifts:

Print Copies:

Ad/Promotions:

Other Costs:

Total Costs:

Book Title: _______________________________

Editing: □

Formatting: □

Cover: □

Promotional Graphics: □

Blog Tours: □

Swag: □

Gifts: □

Print Copies: □

Ad/Promotions: □

Other Costs:

____________________ □   ____________________ □

____________________ □   ____________________ □

____________________ □   ____________________ □

____________________ □   ____________________ □

____________________ □   ____________________ □

Total Costs: □

Book Title: _______________________________

Editing:

Formatting:

Cover:

Promotional Graphics:

Blog Tours:

Swag:

Gifts:

Print Copies:

Ad/Promotions:

Other Costs:

Total Costs:

Book Title: ___________________________________

Editing:

Formatting:

Cover:

Promotional Graphics:

Blog Tours:

Swag:

Gifts:

Print Copies:

Ad/Promotions:

Other Costs:

____

____

____

____

____

____

____

____

____

____

Total Costs:

Book Title: _______________________________

Editing:

Formatting:

Cover:

Promotional Graphics:

Blog Tours:

Swag:

Gifts:

Print Copies:

Ad/Promotions:

Other Costs:

Total Costs:

Book Title: ________________________________

Editing: [ ]

Formatting: [ ]

Cover: [ ]

Promotional Graphics: [ ]

Blog Tours: [ ]

Swag: [ ]

Gifts: [ ]

Print Copies: [ ]

Ad/Promotions: [ ]

Other Costs:

______________ [ ]   ______________ [ ]

______________ [ ]   ______________ [ ]

______________ [ ]   ______________ [ ]

______________ [ ]   ______________ [ ]

______________ [ ]   ______________ [ ]

Total Costs: [ ]

Book Title: _______________________________

Editing:

Formatting:

Cover:

Promotional Graphics:

Blog Tours:

Swag:

Gifts:

Print Copies:

Ad/Promotions:

Other Costs:

Total Costs:

Book Title: _______________________________

Editing:

Formatting:

Cover:

Promotional Graphics:

Blog Tours:

Swag:

Gifts:

Print Copies:

Ad/Promotions:

Other Costs:

Total Costs:

Book Title: _______________________________

Editing: [ ]

Formatting: [ ]

Cover: [ ]

Promotional Graphics: [ ]

Blog Tours: [ ]

Swag: [ ]

Gifts: [ ]

Print Copies: [ ]

Ad/Promotions: [ ]

Other Costs:

____________ [ ]   ____________ [ ]

____________ [ ]   ____________ [ ]

____________ [ ]   ____________ [ ]

____________ [ ]   ____________ [ ]

____________ [ ]   ____________ [ ]

Total Costs: [ ]

Book Title: ______________________________

Editing:

Formatting:

Cover:

Promotional Graphics:

Blog Tours:

Swag:

Gifts:

Print Copies:

Ad/Promotions:

Other Costs:

Total Costs:

Book Title: ________________________________

Editing:

Formatting:

Cover:

Promotional Graphics:

Blog Tours:

Swag:

Gifts:

Print Copies:

Ad/Promotions:

Other Costs:

Total Costs:

Book Title: _______________________________

Editing:

Formatting:

Cover:

Promotional Graphics:

Blog Tours:

Swag:

Gifts:

Print Copies:

Ad/Promotions:

Other Costs:

Total Costs:

Book Title: _______________________________

Editing:

Formatting:

Cover:

Promotional Graphics:

Blog Tours:

Swag:

Gifts:

Print Copies:

Ad/Promotions:

Other Costs:

Total Costs:

Book Title: ______________________________

Editing:

Formatting:

Cover:

Promotional Graphics:

Blog Tours:

Swag:

Gifts:

Print Copies:

Ad/Promotions:

Other Costs:

____

____

____

____

____

____

____

____

____

____

Total Costs:

Book Title: _______________________________

Editing:

Formatting:

Cover:

Promotional Graphics:

Blog Tours:

Swag:

Gifts:

Print Copies:

Ad/Promotions:

Other Costs:

Total Costs:

Book Title: _______________________________

Editing: [ ]

Formatting: [ ]

Cover: [ ]

Promotional Graphics: [ ]

Blog Tours: [ ]

Swag: [ ]

Gifts: [ ]

Print Copies: [ ]

Ad/Promotions: [ ]

Other Costs:

_______________ [ ]   _______________ [ ]

_______________ [ ]   _______________ [ ]

_______________ [ ]   _______________ [ ]

_______________ [ ]   _______________ [ ]

_______________ [ ]   _______________ [ ]

Total Costs: [ ]

Book Title: _______________________________

Editing:

Formatting:

Cover:

Promotional Graphics:

Blog Tours:

Swag:

Gifts:

Print Copies:

Ad/Promotions:

Other Costs:

Total Costs:

Book Title: __________________________

Editing:

Formatting:

Cover:

Promotional Graphics:

Blog Tours:

Swag:

Gifts:

Print Copies:

Ad/Promotions:

Other Costs:

Total Costs:

Book Title: _______________________________

Editing:

Formatting:

Cover:

Promotional Graphics:

Blog Tours:

Swag:

Gifts:

Print Copies:

Ad/Promotions:

Other Costs:

Total Costs:

Book Title: _______________________________

Editing:

Formatting:

Cover:

Promotional Graphics:

Blog Tours:

Swag:

Gifts:

Print Copies:

Ad/Promotions:

Other Costs:

Total Costs:

Book Title: _______________________________

Editing:

Formatting:

Cover:

Promotional Graphics:

Blog Tours:

Swag:

Gifts:

Print Copies:

Ad/Promotions:

Other Costs:

____

____

____

____

____

____

____

____

____

____

Total Costs:

Book Title: ______________________________

Editing:

Formatting:

Cover:

Promotional Graphics:

Blog Tours:

Swag:

Gifts:

Print Copies:

Ad/Promotions:

Other Costs:

Total Costs:

Book Title: ______________________________

Editing:

Formatting:

Cover:

Promotional Graphics:

Blog Tours:

Swag:

Gifts:

Print Copies:

Ad/Promotions:

Other Costs:

Total Costs:

Book Title: _______________________________

Editing:

Formatting:

Cover:

Promotional Graphics:

Blog Tours:

Swag:

Gifts:

Print Copies:

Ad/Promotions:

Other Costs:

Total Costs:

Book Title: ______________________________

Editing:

Formatting:

Cover:

Promotional Graphics:

Blog Tours:

Swag:

Gifts:

Print Copies:

Ad/Promotions:

Other Costs:

Total Costs:

Book Title: _______________________________

Editing:

Formatting:

Cover:

Promotional Graphics:

Blog Tours:

Swag:

Gifts:

Print Copies:

Ad/Promotions:

Other Costs:

Total Costs:

Book Title: _______________________________

Editing:

Formatting:

Cover:

Promotional Graphics:

Blog Tours:

Swag:

Gifts:

Print Copies:

Ad/Promotions:

Other Costs:

Total Costs:

Book Title: ___________________________________

Editing:

Formatting:

Cover:

Promotional Graphics:

Blog Tours:

Swag:

Gifts:

Print Copies:

Ad/Promotions:

Other Costs:

Total Costs:

Book Title: ___________________________

Editing: [ ]

Formatting: [ ]

Cover: [ ]

Promotional Graphics: [ ]

Blog Tours: [ ]

Swag: [ ]

Gifts: [ ]

Print Copies: [ ]

Ad/Promotions: [ ]

Other Costs:

___________ [ ] ___________ [ ]

___________ [ ] ___________ [ ]

___________ [ ] ___________ [ ]

___________ [ ] ___________ [ ]

___________ [ ] ___________ [ ]

Total Costs: [ ]

Book Title: _______________________________

Editing:

Formatting:

Cover:

Promotional Graphics:

Blog Tours:

Swag:

Gifts:

Print Copies:

Ad/Promotions:

Other Costs:

___________	☐	___________	☐
___________	☐	___________	☐
___________	☐	___________	☐
___________	☐	___________	☐
___________	☐	___________	☐

Total Costs: ☐

Book Title: _______________________________

Editing:

Formatting:

Cover:

Promotional Graphics:

Blog Tours:

Swag:

Gifts:

Print Copies:

Ad/Promotions:

Other Costs:

Total Costs:

Book Title: ___________________________________

Editing:

Formatting:

Cover:

Promotional Graphics:

Blog Tours:

Swag:

Gifts:

Print Copies:

Ad/Promotions:

Other Costs:

Total Costs:

Book Title: _______________________________

Editing:

Formatting:

Cover:

Promotional Graphics:

Blog Tours:

Swag:

Gifts:

Print Copies:

Ad/Promotions:

Other Costs:

Total Costs:

Book Title: ___________________________________

Editing: [ ]

Formatting: [ ]

Cover: [ ]

Promotional Graphics: [ ]

Blog Tours: [ ]

Swag: [ ]

Gifts: [ ]

Print Copies: [ ]

Ad/Promotions: [ ]

Other Costs:

_______________	[ ]	_______________	[ ]
_______________	[ ]	_______________	[ ]
_______________	[ ]	_______________	[ ]
_______________	[ ]	_______________	[ ]
_______________	[ ]	_______________	[ ]

Total Costs: [ ]

Book Title: _______________________________

Editing:

Formatting:

Cover:

Promotional Graphics:

Blog Tours:

Swag:

Gifts:

Print Copies:

Ad/Promotions:

Other Costs:

Total Costs:

Book Title: _______________________________

Editing:

Formatting:

Cover:

Promotional Graphics:

Blog Tours:

Swag:

Gifts:

Print Copies:

Ad/Promotions:

Other Costs:

Total Costs:

Book Title: ________________________________

Editing:

Formatting:

Cover:

Promotional Graphics:

Blog Tours:

Swag:

Gifts:

Print Copies:

Ad/Promotions:

Other Costs:

Total Costs:

Book Title: _________________________________

Editing:

Formatting:

Cover:

Promotional Graphics:

Blog Tours:

Swag:

Gifts:

Print Copies:

Ad/Promotions:

Other Costs:

____

____

____

____

____

Total Costs:

Book Title: ______________________________

Editing:

Formatting:

Cover:

Promotional Graphics:

Blog Tours:

Swag:

Gifts:

Print Copies:

Ad/Promotions:

Other Costs:

Total Costs:

Book Title: ________________________________

Editing: [ ]

Formatting: [ ]

Cover: [ ]

Promotional Graphics: [ ]

Blog Tours: [ ]

Swag: [ ]

Gifts: [ ]

Print Copies: [ ]

Ad/Promotions: [ ]

Other Costs:

______________ [ ]   ______________ [ ]

______________ [ ]   ______________ [ ]

______________ [ ]   ______________ [ ]

______________ [ ]   ______________ [ ]

______________ [ ]   ______________ [ ]

Total Costs: [ ]

Book Title: ___________________________

Editing:

Formatting:

Cover:

Promotional Graphics:

Blog Tours:

Swag:

Gifts:

Print Copies:

Ad/Promotions:

Other Costs:

Total Costs:

Book Title: ________________________________

Editing:

Formatting:

Cover:

Promotional Graphics:

Blog Tours:

Swag:

Gifts:

Print Copies:

Ad/Promotions:

Other Costs:

____

____

____

____

____

Total Costs:

Book Title: ______________________________

Editing:

Formatting:

Cover:

Promotional Graphics:

Blog Tours:

Swag:

Gifts:

Print Copies:

Ad/Promotions:

Other Costs:

Total Costs:

Book Title: _________________________________

Editing:

Formatting:

Cover:

Promotional Graphics:

Blog Tours:

Swag:

Gifts:

Print Copies:

Ad/Promotions:

Other Costs:

Total Costs:

Book Title: _______________________________

Editing:

Formatting:

Cover:

Promotional Graphics:

Blog Tours:

Swag:

Gifts:

Print Copies:

Ad/Promotions:

Other Costs:

Total Costs:

Book Title: ___________________________

Editing:

Formatting:

Cover:

Promotional Graphics:

Blog Tours:

Swag:

Gifts:

Print Copies:

Ad/Promotions:

Other Costs:

Total Costs:

Book Title: _______________________________

Editing:

Formatting:

Cover:

Promotional Graphics:

Blog Tours:

Swag:

Gifts:

Print Copies:

Ad/Promotions:

Other Costs:

Total Costs:

Book Title: ______________________________

Editing: [ ]

Formatting: [ ]

Cover: [ ]

Promotional Graphics: [ ]

Blog Tours: [ ]

Swag: [ ]

Gifts: [ ]

Print Copies: [ ]

Ad/Promotions: [ ]

Other Costs:

______________ [ ]   ______________ [ ]

______________ [ ]   ______________ [ ]

______________ [ ]   ______________ [ ]

______________ [ ]   ______________ [ ]

______________ [ ]   ______________ [ ]

Total Costs: [ ]

Book Title: ___________________________________

Editing:

Formatting:

Cover:

Promotional Graphics:

Blog Tours:

Swag:

Gifts:

Print Copies:

Ad/Promotions:

Other Costs:

Total Costs:

Book Title: ___________________________________

Editing:

Formatting:

Cover:

Promotional Graphics:

Blog Tours:

Swag:

Gifts:

Print Copies:

Ad/Promotions:

Other Costs:

Total Costs:

Book Title: _______________________________

Editing:

Formatting:

Cover:

Promotional Graphics:

Blog Tours:

Swag:

Gifts:

Print Copies:

Ad/Promotions:

Other Costs:

Total Costs:

Book Title: ______________________________

Editing:

Formatting:

Cover:

Promotional Graphics:

Blog Tours:

Swag:

Gifts:

Print Copies:

Ad/Promotions:

Other Costs:

Total Costs:

Book Title: _______________________________

Editing:

Formatting:

Cover:

Promotional Graphics:

Blog Tours:

Swag:

Gifts:

Print Copies:

Ad/Promotions:

Other Costs:

Total Costs:

Book Title: _______________________________

Editing:

Formatting:

Cover:

Promotional Graphics:

Blog Tours:

Swag:

Gifts:

Print Copies:

Ad/Promotions:

Other Costs:

Total Costs:

Book Title: ___________________________________

Editing:

Formatting:

Cover:

Promotional Graphics:

Blog Tours:

Swag:

Gifts:

Print Copies:

Ad/Promotions:

Other Costs:

Total Costs:

Book Title: ______________________________

Editing:

Formatting:

Cover:

Promotional Graphics:

Blog Tours:

Swag:

Gifts:

Print Copies:

Ad/Promotions:

Other Costs:

Total Costs:

Book Title: _______________________________

Editing:

Formatting:

Cover:

Promotional Graphics:

Blog Tours:

Swag:

Gifts:

Print Copies:

Ad/Promotions:

Other Costs:

____

____

____

____

____

Total Costs:

Book Title: _______________________________

Editing:

Formatting:

Cover:

Promotional Graphics:

Blog Tours:

Swag:

Gifts:

Print Copies:

Ad/Promotions:

Other Costs:

Total Costs:

Thank you so much for your purchase.

I really do hope that this book has helped you,
even in some small way.

Would you like to see different designs/styles?

I am always very happy to hear from customers,
so please feel free to email me on

teeceedesignstudio@yahoo.com